796.332 Sto
Stowers, Carlton
Texas football legends :
   greats of the game

$8.95
ocn213480072
10/23/2008

Texas Football Legends

Texas Football Legends
Greats of the Game

by Carlton Stowers

TCU PRESS • FORT WORTH
A TEXAS SMALL BOOK ★

Library of Congress Cataloging-in-Publication Data
Stowers, Carlton.
Texas football legends : greats of the game / Carlton Stowers.
p.cm. - (Texas Small Books)
ISBN 978-0-87565-376-1 (cloth : alk. paper)
1. Football players--Texas--Biography. I.Title.
GV939.A1S76 2008
796.3320922--dc22
[B]
2008011546

TCU Press
P. O. Box 298300
Fort Worth, Texas 76129
817.257.7822
http://www.prs.tcu.edu

To order books: 800.826.8911

Printed in China by Everbest through
Four Colour Imports, Ltd., Louisville, Kentucky

Design: Margie Adkins Graphic Design

For Bill Stevens

. . . who will quickly question
why there aren't more old Aggies

Contents

Preface

Lists have always fascinated me. I'm an absolute, flat-out, unapologetic sucker for them. Pick the Best Chicken Fried Steak Restaurants or All-Time Great Movies, Top Ten Doo-Wop Songs or publish the *New York Times'* Bestsellers and you've got my unbridled attention.

When asked to write this little book, listing Texas' Greatest Texas Football Players, I jumped at the opportunity with no thought given to the hazards of the exercise. Still, the space assigned me provided a tight squeeze. Better I'd been asked to tell you about the Top 50. Maybe more. Which is something of a backdoor apology. Those who have gone unmentioned would make a dandy All-Star team. Or two.

But, a short list of elite players it is. They're my picks and I'm sticking to 'em. It is as fair a selection as personal bias will allow. Had Texas sportswriting legends like Blackie Sherrod or Dan Jenkins or Mickey Herskowitz made the picks, the team picture would have no doubt been different. Same with Joe Fan down the block.

Still, I'll play them with this group and spot them a touchdown.

Finally, as you grumble at omission of your favorite player, be aware that this book is not a product of rocket science. No computers were used in the selection process. The only hard and fast rule I opted for was that each of those profiled were native Texans. Which is why you'll find no quarterback named Staubach or Heisman Trophy winner named Dorsett mentioned. To learn more about them you'll have to check Best lists compiled in Ohio and Pennsylvania. ★

Carlton Stowers

Doak Walker

The story, as it has been handed down over the years, played out in a small drug store near the Southern Methodist University campus. A sports-minded shopper lingered at the magazine rack for several minutes before making his selection. No sooner had he done so, SMU running back Kyle Rote approached and politely warned him against his purchase. "You don't want that one," Rote warned. "It isn't official. It doesn't have Doak Walker's picture on the cover."

Indeed, in that football season of 1948, Ewell Doak Walker had been elevated to the college football equivalent of a modern day rock star, appearing on no less than 47 magazine covers, including *Life, Look* and *Colliers.* He was—and remains—the most celebrated and honored player in the storied history of Texas football.

Son of school-teaching parents, Walker hinted of what was to come when he was picked to All-District and All-State teams while playing halfback for Highland Park High School. Then, attending college just a few blocks from home, he kicked his career into high gear. He was a four-time All-Southwest Conference selection. Three times he was a consensus All-America tailback, his running, passing and punting leading SMU to national prominence. Twice he led the Mustangs to Cotton Bowl appearances, earning MVP honors in both games. As a junior he received the Heisman Trophy, awarded to the nation's premier collegiate player, to add to the prestigious Maxwell Trophy he'd earned the previous season.

Though injured much of his senior year, he learned that he was again being considered by *Collier's* for its annual post-season All-America team. The modest Walker wrote a letter to the magazine's sports editor, Bill Fay, asking that his name be removed from consideration. The magazine responded by putting Walker on its cover and naming him the Player of the Year—for Sportsmanship.

So vested was Dallas in the Saturday heroics of Walker that it became necessary to move home games from the SMU campus stadium to the 30,000-seat Cotton Bowl. Such were game day crowds that the decision to expand the seating capacity of the storied Dallas stadium was made prior to Walker's junior season. In time, they would refer to it as "The House That Doak Built."

During his four years at SMU, Walker amassed 3,862 yards in total offense and scored 303 points. Additionally, he accounted for 1,500 yards on kick returns and nearly 500 yards receiving. He punted for a 39-yard average and intercepted 12 passes.

Ultimately he would be included on *Sports Illustrated's* All-Century collegiate team and enshrined in the College Football Hall of Fame.

"Doak Walker came along in an era when everyone was looking for heroes," recalled former SMU teammate Dick Davis. "In those post-World War II days, folks were looking for something good to focus their attention on. And Walker filled the bill. He truly was what an All-American should be. He was a complete athlete and a complete gentleman. He made good grades and was one of the most popular figures on campus, in the community and with his teammates. I grew up with the guy, played high school football with him, and he was a hero to me."

Still, for all his remarkable collegiate glories, there were those who doubted the 5'10," 168-pound Walker had much of a future in the professional ranks when he joined old schoolboy teammate Bobby Layne as a member of the Detroit Lions. Doak quickly disproved the critics, earning Rookie of the Year honors in 1950. Before his five-year pro career was completed, he had made the All-Pro team on four occasions, twice led the NFL in scoring, and helped the Lions to two league championships. In time he would join Layne in the NFL Hall of Fame.

"You know," said former Detroit teammate Cloyce Box, "I was several years older than Doak, but when he arrived at training camp his rookie year I was literally awed by him and his incredible collegiate career. I remember being astonished that he was so down-to-earth, so modest. There wasn't an ounce of prima donna in him. Just the opposite. He went out, did his job every Sunday, then passed the credit around to everyone else."

"He was," said Layne during Walker's induction into the Pro Football Hall of Fame, "a guy who always made the big play when you needed it. More than that, you knew he was going to do it."

Rote, who as a young collegian had warned that magazine buyer about any publication that failed to make Walker its cover boy, told Witt Channing, author of *Doak Walker: More Than a Hero,* "The first thing that comes to mind about Doak is that he is one of the most decent people I ever knew. I never heard him say anything bad

3

about anyone, friend or foe. He was a great team player and an inspiration to everyone around him. And I guess 'I' was the least-used word in his vocabulary."

Such is the stuff of which icons are made.

Today, the nation's premier college running backs annually battle for a coveted trophy awarded to the best of the best at season's end: the Doak Walker Award. The winner has large shoes to fill. ★

Sammy Baugh

There is a certain majesty to the name: Samuel Adrian Baugh. It would have been perfectly fitting for a beloved elder statesman, perhaps a military genius, even an acclaimed man of letters. It rings with that rare musical class befitting one destined to become a national hero. But to sports writers, a breed rarely given to leaving well enough alone, the sheer melody would not suffice.

For one so gifted, an athlete of such trendsetting bent, there simply had to be a nickname.

Thus you know him best as "Slingin' Sam," the lanky raw-boned Texan who ushered a new kind of offensive excitement to the Southwest Conference in the late '30s; the man who, despite passage of well over a half century since those golden days when he led the TCU Horned Frogs to national prominence and the Washington Redskins to professional success, remains one of the most warmly remembered quarterbacks ever to play the game.

His list of accomplishments is endless: A two-time All-American, he directed TCU to victory in the 1936 Sugar Bowl and a year later helped inaugurate the Cotton

Bowl with a victory over Marquette. As a professional, Baugh led the NFL in passing six times, played in five NFL championship games, winning twice. A charter member of pro football's Hall of Fame, he still holds numerous league passing, punting and defensive records.

Not bad for a guy who never wanted anything more than to one day be a major league baseball third baseman.

It was no small disappointment to Baugh when he learned that Sweetwater High School, where he would play football and basketball in his senior year after the family moved from East Texas, did not field a baseball team. To fill his springtime void, young Baugh regularly drove to nearby Abilene where he played for a semi-pro team.

"That year," Baugh remembers, "we played a game against TCU and beat them. I had a pretty good game and the TCU coach told me he'd like for me to think about coming to school there."

Just a week later, however, legendary University of Texas coach Billy Disch came calling with a similar offer.

Choosing to attend UT, Baugh immediately began practicing with the baseball team but couldn't help notice that candidates for the Longhorns football team were working out nearby. "I'd go sit in the stands and watch them after we got through with our practice," he said, "and it dawned on me pretty quickly that I wasn't ready to give up football."

Baugh left Austin for Fort Worth and TCU.

There, Dutch Meyer, an innovative Horned Frogs coach, quickly designed a sped-up offense that relied heavily on a short passing game—and the new kid from Sweetwater was the perfect triggerman.

During his tenure as the starting TCU quarterback, Baugh led the Frogs to 29 victories and threw for 3,471 yards and 39 touchdowns.

Following his senior year Baugh was the No. 1 draft pick of the NFL Washington Redskins and signed a contract that would earn him the regal sum of $8,000 for his rookie season.

Yet even as his football career continued to blossom, Baugh still thought about playing baseball. In 1937, after leading Washington to the NFL title, he joined the St. Louis Cardinals in the spring and spent a season playing shortstop in the minor leagues. "I'd been playing third base since I was 12 years old and knew I'd never make it to the big leagues at short," he said.

Thus he returned to football the following fall. Before his career would end after the 1952 season, he re-wrote the NFL record book, not just with his passing and punting (in 1940 he averaged a titanic 51.4 yards per punt; for his career he averaged a record 45.1) and his defensive play (in one game he accomplished a record-tying four interceptions).

Following his retirement, he coached first at Hardin-Simmons University in Abilene, then with the New York Titans of the newly-formed American Football League. ★

Earl Campbell

His speech is slow and measured, an easy-flowing East Texas drawl one might expect from someone working on his third after-work highball. Be advised, however, that Earl Christian Campbell, former All-American and All-Pro, Heisman Trophy winner and member of the Pro Football Hall of Fame, does not imbibe.

In fact, the University of Texas legend may be the only person since Austin's Prohibition heyday to be asked to leave a popular off-campus night spot for committing the unpardonable sin of ordering three consecutive glasses of straight orange juice. "Sir," a waitress finally informed him, "I'm sorry, but the manager has asked us to suggest to people that they leave after a while if they're not drinking alcoholic beverages."

In view of his muscular 6'1," 220-pound frame and widespread reputation for knocking defensive linemen bleary since his schoolboy days at John Tyler High School, Campbell's decision to quietly move on had to be a great relief to the watering hole's management. "It was no big deal," he says, reflecting on the long-ago event. "A friend of mine from Tyler was in town and wanted to see a little of the Austin night life. That was the only reason I was there in the first place."

Even then the young man nicknamed the Tyler Rose, the sixth of 11 children, had a laser-like focus on his future. He might have been a speech and communications major at Texas, but Earl Campbell knew his future was as a football player. "The Lord," he reflects, "blesses all of us

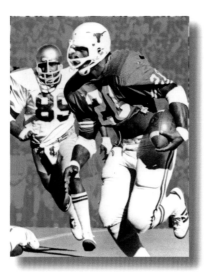

with a special gift, and He expects us to use it. My gift was to play football and it was always important to me to be the very best I could at it." It was a Southern Baptist philosophy that carried him to incredible heights.

After Campbell had led his high school team to the state Class AAAA championship, University of Oklahoma coach Barry Switzer, unsuccessful in recruiting Earl to play for his Sooners, remarked that he was the only schoolboy player he'd ever seen who could have bypassed college football and gone directly to the professional ranks and become an immediate success.

You'll pardon the cliché but, as a collegian, he was a man among boys. During his career at UT, Campbell rushed for 4,444 yards and scored 41 touchdowns and was

9

twice a consensus All-America selection. Then, at the end of the 1977 season came college football's top honor: the Heisman.

It is not, however, Campbell's game day performances and accolades that former coach Darrell Royal best remembers. "Earl was the most serious young man I was ever around," he insists. "There was never room for nonsense in his life. He was too busy making something of himself."

That mindset didn't change when the Houston Oilers made him the first player selected in the 1978 NFL draft, or when he was cited as the league's Rookie of the Year and Most Valuable Player on six occasions, or when, year after year, he was an All-Pro and Pro Bowl selection.

Campbell's rare combination of speed and power enabled him to lead the NFL in rushing three consecutive years (1978-79-80), a feat matched only by fellow Hall of Famer and legendary Cleveland running back Jim Brown. "Earl," says Brown, "accomplished the things he did while carrying a tremendous load. He was called on to do it all; the man they looked to for short yardage first downs or to break the long gain, the touchdowns, everything. To do what he did required him to go full speed at all times, on every play. For him to have done that year after year was remarkable."

During his eight-year professional career (the last with the New Orleans Saints where he was reunited with former Oilers coach Bum Phillips), Campbell accumulated 9,407 yards rushing and scored 74 touchdowns. In 1980 alone he had four 200-yard rushing games enroute to a career single season high 1,934 yards.

And his status as a favorite son of Texas was forever sealed in 1981 when the state legislature proclaimed him an Official State Hero, an honor previously awarded only to historical figures Davy Crockett, Stephen F. Austin and Sam Houston. In 2006, a statue of Campbell was unveiled in a corner of Royal Memorial Stadium. ★

Bob Lilly

He was, throughout an All-America collegiate career and All-Pro stardom in the NFL, one of those who played the game with remarkably somber control.

Bob Lilly went about his job as one of the game's most destructive defensive linemen with a single-minded, finely focused approach. He played with an intensity that was off the charts.

All that said, however, Lilly is a man for whom the game was always a highly emotional endeavor. And when he did allow those personal feelings to show through, the moments were memorable.

In a banquet room in Dallas, during ceremonies that would have him inducted into the Southwest Conference Hall of Honor, he encountered one of the most emotional times of his athletic life.

"I very nearly broke down," he says, "thinking of the Southwest Conference disbanding. It had been such an important part of my life since I was just a kid."

There is a warmth in his voice as he recalls listening to the immortal Kern Tips calling the Humble Game of the Week on the tiny Philco in the living room of his family's Throckmorton home. He remembers traveling to Fort Worth in the company of his farmer father to watch the TCU Horned Frogs play on bygone autumn Saturdays.

"When TCU offered me a scholarship," he says, "it meant more to me than the opportunity to wear the purple and white uniform and play for a school I'd been such a fan of. It meant I was going to be a part of the Southwest Conference."

And the 6'6," 200-pound lineman made the most of the opportunity, first earning all-conference honors, then being a consensus All-American.

It was in his senior year of 1960 that nearby Dallas was dealt a franchise by the National Football League powers that be. The newly-formed Cowboys wasted little time making him their first round draft selection.

As his spectacular pro career, all 14 years of it spent with Dallas, was winding to an end, drawing him closer to the day he would be summoned to the National Football League Hall of Fame, Bob Lilly never wished for a return to

the hard time early years of the growing franchise. Rarely, in fact, did he ever speak nostalgically of the infant days of the Cowboys when he was the cornerstone upon which the team's defense would be built.

"When it was getting about time for me to retire," he remembers, "people would ask me if I ever wished I could start my career all over again. The question always amused me.

"In the latter stages of my playing days I was rarely hurt, for the simple reason I knew what I was doing. My first year in the NFL was a little different story. That (1961) season I broke five ribs, a wrist, a thumb, hurt my knee and twisted both ankles."

The fact that he earned a spot on the NFL All-Rookie team that season as a defensive end, a position at which he never felt comfortable, hardly overshadowed the pain and frustration of those hardscrabble times.

Through those early, struggling years, Lilly stood as proof that there was hope for the Cowboys' future. Seven times he was an All-Pro selection, the first player inducted into Texas Stadium's Ring of Honor and was the first from the franchise to be named to the Hall of Fame.

When the Cowboys finally managed to win their first Super Bowl it was Bob Lilly who celebrated most enthusiastically, understanding, perhaps better than any other member of the team the significance of a world championship.

It is no surprise, then, that the game which remains most vivid in his mind is the one in which Dallas first accomplished a goal it had been working toward for over a decade.

"I can think back to some pretty doggy days during those early expansion years," he says, "as well as some pretty high times, like winning our first Eastern Conference championship in 1966. There were some gripping disappointments even in that era, though: losing to a couple of great Green Bay teams in '66 and '67 and the sick feeling of losing to Baltimore in our first trip to the Super Bowl in 1970."

The Cowboys, the critics howled, had become a team of great talent but simply weren't able to win the big one. "Next Year's Champions," as sportswriter Steve Perkins labeled them.

"For that reason, if nothing else, the game I'll still be able to call to memory years and years from now will be our Super Bowl victory over the Miami Dolphins. On that day—January 16, 1972—the Cowboys set to rest a lot of conversation about our previous failures. That 24-3 victory was far more than a big payday and a ring to me.

"I still can't really describe the feeling that comes from winning a Super Bowl. It's something you can only share with the players and coaches on your team. I can only say that it was the greatest thrill of my playing career.

"After that game our dressing room was a madhouse. Tom Landry's face was one big smile—and I don't have to tell you how unusual that was—and everyone was slapping each other on the back. Someone gave me a cigar and I lit it up. I've never been happier—for my teammates, for myself, and for Coach Landry." ★

Bobby Layne

Downstairs, only the whistling of a slow-moving janitor broke the early morning silence. The bank was still blanketed in the semi-darkness its tinted windows afforded, and outside parking spaces were still in abundance. On the eighth floor of Lubbock's Citizen's Tower, however, life moved at a far more rapid pace. Laughter escaped from Suite 802 as the door stood ajar.

Inside, a stout, blue-eyed businessman, leaning back in a huge leather chair fit for a high-ranking politician, was sipping from a cup of coffee and talking on the phone to a friend long accustomed to hearing from him in those hours before the alarm clock officially signaled the new day.

Bobby Layne was arranging his annual fishing trip to Mexico. The men he would lead on the expedition were the same he had led on football fields in Detroit and Pittsburgh two decades earlier.

He wasn't asking if they wanted to go. Rather, he was simply telling them when and where they were going. Layne was, long after his Hall of Fame career, still calling the plays.

By then slowed by two surgeries for throat cancer and a cataract operation which severely affected the sight in one eye, Layne continued to live life in high gear until his death.

Doctors had told him to slow down and get more rest. And for a while he tried to follow the orders. But in time he returned to old habits and rested less than ever. He had too many things to do.

He made a concerted effort to fill his days with good times, organizing charity golf tournaments, attending team reunions, bird hunting with his beloved English Springer Spaniel, Duke, fishing, quick weekend trips to Las Vegas to try and beat another kind of odds and visiting with old Highland Park High schoolmate Doak Walker.

Before all was said and done, Layne had collected every honor that awaits those who climb to the highest rank in the game of football. There was not a hall of fame from Michigan to Texas that had not honored him with induction. He had championship rings and All-Pro citations. He had smiled from the cover of *Time* magazine.

"I never met a man," says Ernie Stautner, a Pittsburgh

Steelers teammate, "who so many people considered their best friend."

During a career which was to see him earn All-Southwest Conference and All-American honors at the University of Texas to two NFL championships during his 15 years in the professional ranks, Layne earned the reputation of a winner despite the fact his passes were usually a bit wobbly and his foot speed at best modest. Said longtime friend Walker, who was reunited with Layne as a member of the Detroit Lions, "Bobby never lost a game; time just ran out on him occasionally."

"He was the greatest competitor I've ever seen perform," said former University of Texas roommate Rooster Andrews of the Santa Anna, Texas-born youngster who was raised by an aunt and uncle.

Andrews pointed to the 1946 Cotton Bowl game that matched Layne's UT Longhorns against the University of Missouri. On that New Year's Day, Layne, just a sophomore at the time, had a hand in every point scored as Texas won, 40-27. He scored four touchdowns, passed for two others, and kicked four extra points.

Two years later, as an All-American senior, he was named the outstanding player in the Sugar Bowl following Texas' defeat of Alabama.

In the spring, Layne turned his attention to baseball. As a pitcher for the Longhorns he won 28 consecutive games, never suffering defeat.

It was in the professional football arena, however, that the Layne legend grew. One of the last NFL players to refuse the use of a face mask, he was twice an All-Pro selection while leading the Lions to three divisional titles and two league championships. By the time he completed his career with a four-year stay as the Pittsburgh Steelers' quarterback, he had established NFL career records for most passes attempted and completed, yards gained passing and touchdown passes thrown.

In the 1953 NFL championship game, the Cleveland Browns led Detroit, 16-10, with just over four minutes left to play. Layne gathered his team into the huddle and said, "Just follow ol' Bobby and we'll win this thing." Layne then directed the team on a methodical 80-yard touchdown drive and Walker's extra point kick gave the Lions a 17-16 win.

No sooner were his playing days over than the honors flowed. Layne has been enshrined in the College Football Hall of Fame, the Pro Football Hall of Fame, the University of Texas' Longhorn Hall of Fame, Cotton Bowl Hall of Fame, as well as numerous others throughout Texas, Michigan and Pennsylvania. In a 1995 special edition devoted to the all-time greats of pro football, *Sports Illustrated* called Layne "The Toughest Quarterback Who Ever Lived."

And that remarkable determination to win never faded, even long after he'd played his last game.

In 1967, Layne coached a team of Texas high school all-stars who traveled to Hershey, Pennsylvania, to play the best schoolboys from Pennsylvania in what was called the Big 33 game. His Texans scored a resounding 42-14 victory. ★

Davey O'Brien

He was a little man assigned to fill big shoes. Long and tall Sammy Baugh, the strong-armed quarterback who brought the passing game to prominence in college football, had completed his eligibility at Texas Christian University and gone off to the NFL. Left behind was a successor who stood only 5'7" and weighed 151 pounds.

Yet Davey O'Brien played the game like a giant,

accomplishing things no TCU quarterback, before or since, has. In 1938, his senior year, he led the Horned Frogs to an undefeated season and the school's lone national championship. By the time he threw a touchdown pass and kicked a field goal to lead the way past Carnegie Tech, the premier team in the East, in the season-ending Sugar Bowl, Robert David O'Brien had been picked to no less than 13 All-American teams and became the first college football player to win the Heisman Trophy, Maxwell Trophy and Walter Camp Award as the nation's top performer in the same year. To this day he is the smallest player ever to receive the awards.

Imagine what he might have done had he been 6'3" and 220.

To celebrate his winning the Heisman, appreciative TCU boosters hired a horse-drawn stagecoach to transport him from his Manhattan hotel to New York's Downtown Athletic Club where the presentation was to be made. And, why not a bit of Texas showmanship? That's what Lil' Davey had been producing week after week during his final collegiate season.

He had set a Southwest Conference passing record with 1,457 yards, a mark that would stand for a decade, threw for 19 touchdowns and set an NCAA record for most passes and runs in a single season—400. For good measure, he handled the Horned Frogs' punting and place kicking duties.

Still, there was, to be honest, little cause to see such celestial heroics coming. At Dallas' Woodrow Wilson High, O'Brien had been an All-State performer and led his team into the playoffs. But, he weighed only 118 pounds. Most college water boys were bigger. Still, TCU coach Dutch Meyer invited the young Dallas-born athlete to Fort Worth. Few were surprised when he spent most of his early years on the bench, watching upperclassman Baugh set passing records. When, as a junior in 1937, O'Brien moved into the starting quarterback job and led a team that posted only a 4-4-2 record, there was hardly reason to believe that great days were just around the corner.

And, while his offensive production as a runner, passer and kicker were generally enough to win the day, O'Brien occasionally found more inventive ways to keep the Horned Frogs unbeaten through a 10-game regular season. On a Saturday afternoon when rival SMU trailed by only a touchdown and threatened to upset the Horned Frogs, O'Brien returned a punt 39 yards to set up his 37-yard touchdown pass and put the game out of reach. Result: a 20-7 TCU win.

By the time his win-it-all senior season was completed, even the size-conscious NFL was convinced the swift, strong-armed O'Brien was the real thing. The Philadelphia Eagles drafted him, offering a $10,000-per-season salary. The young Texan earned every penny of it.

As a rookie he passed for 1,324 yards, erasing a first-year NFL mark previously held by former TCU teammate Baugh, and earned All-Pro honors. The achievements earned him a $2,000 raise. His second professional season, however, would be his last. In his final game on December 1, 1940, O'Brien was matched with old teammate Baugh and the Washington Redskins. The Redskins would win but O'Brien set NFL records that day as he threw 60 passes, completing 33 for 316 yards.

Then the Eagles quarterback announced his retirement.

His football career completed, he joined the Federal Bureau of Investigation and, after being sworn in as a special agent, served a lengthy stint as a field agent in Springfield, Missouri. He later returned to the Academy in Quantico where he became the Bureau's firearms instructor. He ended his FBI career in the field office of his hometown of Dallas.

And, long after he'd thrown his final pass, the honors continued. In 1955, he was inducted into the National Foundation Football Hall of Fame. A year later the Texas Sports Hall of Fame honored him.

Diagnosed with cancer in 1971, O'Brien died in November 1977. His legacy, however, would live on. Just a month after his death the Fort Worth Club presented its first Davey O'Brien Award. Today the trophy, a bronze replica of the man for whom it is named, is annually awarded to that college quarterback judged the best in the nation.

The shoes filled by each year's new winner are big ones. ★

Vince Young

There are magical moments, frozen in time, that clearly define the public's fascination with sports. One such occurred on a late California evening in January of 2006. The setting was the historic Rose Bowl game, matching No.1-ranked Southern Cal, a team with a 34-game winning streak, against second-ranked Texas, a team which had completed the regular season 11-0. The winner would be declared college football's premier team.

Throughout the evening, USC, powered by quarterback Matt Leinart and running back Reggie Bush, both Heisman Trophy winners, demonstrated why their team was not only the defending national champion but, quite possibly, the finest ever to play the game. Vince Young, a 6'5", 233-pound University of Texas quarterback, wasn't buying it. The Houston native spent the evening baffling the USC defense as he passed for 267 yards and ran for 200 more in what many would label the most incredible single game performance ever witnessed.

Still, with only 19 seconds showing on the clock, the Trojans led. Until, on a desperation fourth down play, Young raced into the end zone from nine yards out to hand Texas a 41-38 victory. And in that moment, the national championship was passed to the Longhorns, Young was voted the game's Most Valuable Player, and in his hometown Houston "Vince Young Day" was proclaimed, adding new chapters to Vincent Paul Young, Jr.'s résumé.

That legend had begun in a rough-and-tumble neighborhood when Young was a multi-sport schoolboy standout, averaging 25 points per game in basketball, running on the district champion sprint relay in track, and playing in the outfield on the baseball team. As the quarterback for Houston's Madison High, he earned a place on *Parade's* prep All-America team and was named the National Player of the Year by *Student Sports* following a senior season in which he'd led his team to the state finals, accounting for 3,819 yards and 59 touchdowns along the way.

College recruiters from throughout the nation came running to visit the gifted young man who was being raised by his mother and grandmother while his father served time in prison. Ultimately, the University of Texas was his choice; a decision that promised all the ingredients for the perfect storm that would roar full-blast on that historic night in Pasadena.

Coach Mack Brown and his staff had re-designed the Longhorns' offense into a wide-open spread formation attack to better display Young's talents and the decision paid off quickly. In his sophomore year he led UT to an

11-1 season that ended with the team ranked No. 5 in the nation and victorious in its first visit to the Rose Bowl. In a dramatic victory over Big Ten champion Michigan, Young scored four rushing touchdowns and passed for a fifth and was named the game's MVP. During the season he had routinely displayed his dual-threat talents, rushing for 1,189 yards and passing for 1,849. A prime example of his magical touch came in a Big 12 game in which Oklahoma State had bullied its way into a 35-7 lead. Under Young's direction, Texas fashioned a remarkable second half comeback to triumph, 56-35.

The stage, then, was properly set for his fairy tale junior year. In addition to directing the undefeated Longhorns to the national championship, Young would end the regular season as an All-American selection, the nation's top-rated passer, and finish second to USC running back Bush in the Heisman balloting.

And with that he went in search of new worlds to conquer. Choosing to bypass his senior year of eligibility at Texas, Young entered the NFL draft and was the first round selection of the Tennessee Titans, signing a multi-million dollar contract. Still, there were skeptics who doubted that he could star at the professional level with his unorthodox side-armed passing delivery and injury-promising inclination to run with the ball.

Once again, Young quieted the doubters. Earning the starting job with the Titans in his first year, he led his team to a series of come-from-behind victories, setting a new NFL record for rushing yardage by a rookie quarterback (552) along the way. By season's end he was named the league's Rookie of the Year and earned an invitation to the Pro Bowl. ★

John Kimbrough

Youngsters of a bygone generation generally found their heroes either on the nation's football fields or down at the Bijou on Saturday afternoon where B-western movies were the regular fare. A bigger-than-life figure named John Kimbrough fulfilled all needs.

As a hard-running fullback for Texas A&M, he was twice picked to All-America teams. In his junior year of 1939, he was the driving force of an Aggie team that went undefeated and won the mythical national championship. A year later, Jarrin' John was runner-up to Michigan's famed Tom Harmon in the Heisman Trophy balloting.

Next came a chance meeting with Hollywood talent scout Everett Crosby, older brother of crooner Bing, who felt Kimbrough's

square-jawed good looks and Texas swagger were just what the fans of the Saturday afternoon shoot-'em-ups were looking for. Next stop, starring roles in *Sundown Jim* and *Lone Star Ranger*.

But the popcorn nostalgia gets us ahead of our story. Long before Kimbrough sat in Darryl Zanuck's office and agreed to a $1,500-per-week movie contract, became an item in Hedda Hopper's gossip column or hob-nobbed with starlets, he was already a full-blown celebrity back in his home state.

Born and raised in the West Texas community of Haskell, his heroics as a swift, hard-running Aggie fullback were legendary. In 1939 and '40, A&M won 20 of the 21 games it played, losing only to Texas, 7-0, in Kimbrough's senior year. Chief among the reasons was the 6'2," 210-pound fullback's ability to bull his way through and past would-be tacklers. Homer Norton, A&M coach at the time, compared his prized All-American to such football legends as Jim Thorpe, Red Grange and Bronko Nagurski.

The Aggies' 14-13 Sugar Bowl victory over Tulane that ended an undefeated season and sealed the '39 national championship served as a perfect example of Kimbrough's prowess. On that day he rushed 152 yards, scored both of his team's touchdowns, and then, for good measure, blocked a Tulane extra point attempt that would have tied the game and ruined A&M's proud 11-0 season.

And there was a subplot to that remarkable performance. Recruited by Tulane following his high school graduation, Kimbrough actually began his collegiate career at the New Orleans university. There, however, coach Lowell (Red) Dawson was dead set on having him play in the offensive line. Kimbrough said thanks but no thanks, took his leave, and went to A&M.

But, revenge, Kimbrough would later assure author Mickey Herskowitz, played no part in his Sugar Bowl performance. "By then," he said, "I'd forgotten the Tulane coach's name."

Neither did he spend time bemoaning the fact Michigan's Harmon edged him out for the Heisman at the end of that 1940 season in which the Aggies had been ranked No. 1 in the nation most of the year. Others, however, were less charitable, offering the suggestion that since TCU quarterback Davey O'Brien had received the honor in 1938, voters were reluctant to award college football's most coveted prized to another Texas player so soon. It is worth noting that author Dan Jenkins, an astute student of college football history, once wrote that by all rights Kimbrough should have won the Heisman at the end of his magnificent junior season. Instead the award went to Iowa's Nile Kinnick.

Despite having signed a contract to play professionally with the New York Yankees of the All-America

Conference, Kimbrough, though having never so much as acted in a school play, opted to make movies instead of touchdowns.

The slow-talking Texan would debut as the lead in Zane Grey's *Lone Star Ranger.*

"I remember that they had this speech teacher working with me when we started the picture. He was a foreigner and wanted to make me put a little block of wood between my teeth and say, 'how-now-brown-cow,' stuff like that. I finally asked him where he was from and he said he'd come to the U.S. from Hungary. Then I asked how long he'd been speaking English. He told me for just a couple of years; that he'd learned it in some university over there. So, I told him I'd been speaking it all my life and damned well didn't need some foreigner to teach me.

"That was the end of my speech lessons."

And the movie career would abruptly end on the day the Japanese bombed Pearl Harbor, setting the stage for World War II. Having graduated from Texas A&M as a commissioned officer, Kimbrough hurriedly wrapped up filming of his second movie and left Hollywood behind to serve as a pilot in the Army Air Corps.

Discharged with the rank of captain, he signed a contract to play pro football with the Los Angeles Dons in 1946. Following a three-year career during which his passion for the game had begun to wane, he retired and re-turned with his wife Barbara to his hometown of Haskell.

There, he tended his ranch, occasionally traveled to banquets to be honored with induction into the College Football Hall of Fame and the Texas Sports Hall of Fame.

On more leisurely days he'd drive over to visit with long-time friend Sammy Baugh, the legendary TCU and Washington Redskins quarterback, who resided in nearby Rotan. They would drink coffee, play golf and reminisce.

In 1953, Kimbrough briefly entered the political arena, serving a term as a member of the Texas Legislature.

Tommy Nobis

It was one of those moments that provides a screaming exclamation point to one's athletic career. The scene was the 1965 Orange Bowl matching national powers Texas and Alabama. The Longhorns, just a season removed from having won a national championship, were clinging desperately to a 21-17 lead as the final seconds ticked away. The Crimson Tide, led by celebrated quarterback Joe Namath, was just a fourth-down-and-inches away from scoring the go-ahead touchdown. In the huddle, Namath had called a quarterback sneak.

Moments later a thundering collision that would echo into college football history occurred. Junior linebacker Tommy Nobis, Texas' two-time All-America selection, fought off blockers to stop Namath before he could make his way into the end zone. The Longhorns' victory was preserved and another chapter in the growing Nobis legend was written.

By the time he'd played the final game of his

collegiate career, the young San Antonio native had brilliantly filled the role University of Texas head coach Darrell Royal had planned for him. Back in the early '60s, Royal and his staff felt their Longhorns had reached a plateau where, with only one added ingredient, they could legitimately challenge for a national title. That missing piece of the puzzle was a game-controlling middle linebacker, a gifted player like Nobis, who had just completed an All-State career at his hometown Thomas Jefferson High.

By the time he was Texas' lone sophomore starter in that undefeated championship season of 1963, with honors like the Maxwell Trophy (as college football's best player), the Outland Trophy (for best interior lineman) and the Knute Rockne Award (for best lineman) still to come, the 6'3," 230-pound Nobis was being hailed as one of college football history's best. He would steadily add to that reputation throughout his tenure as a Longhorn.

Those, understand, were the pre-specialist days when athletes were still being called on to play both offense and defense. Thus, in addition to his outstanding play as a linebacker, averaging 20 tackles per game through his career, Nobis, a three-time All-Southwest Conference selection, also served as a hole-punching guard in the offensive line. "He was," says Royal, "the finest two-way player I've ever seen."

And, for all the high school and collegiate honors that came his way, Nobis was just getting started.

In the 1966 National Football League draft, the expansion Atlanta Falcons made him the first player selected. The rival American Football League held its own draft and again Nobis' name was the first called (by the Houston Oilers).

The concern over where Nobis would cast his lot reached from nationwide barbershops and watering holes to outer space. Astronaut Frank Borman, aboard Gemini 7 on the eve of the drafts, radioed a message to Mission Control: "Tell Nobis to sign with Houston," he advised.

Instead, he became the first-ever member of the start-up Falcons. And, some still say, the greatest player in the franchise's history. In his first year of professional football, Nobis was named Rookie of the Year and earned an invitation to the Pro Bowl.

There's an oft-repeated story that Falcons coach Norm Van Brocklin, while giving a tour of the team dressing room, pointed to Nobis' locker. "There," he supposedly said, "is where our team dresses."

While Atlanta's won-lost record was year-after-year dismal, the Texas standout chiseled himself a place in NFL history. During his 11-year career, he led the Falcons in tackles nine times, was picked to the Pro Bowl five times and was twice named All-Pro. When the league selected an All-Decade Team for the '60s, Nobis was a member.

His jersey number 60 was the first ever to be retired by the Falcons.

Long after his playing days had ended, Nobis remains a member of the Falcons organization, serving as vice-president of corporate development. In 1975 he founded the Tommy Nobis Center in Atlanta, an organization that provides disabled youths and adults with job training and employment services. For his off-the-field work, he was honored as the NFL Man of the Year.

And the accolades continue. He has been elected to the College Football Hall of Fame as well as the Texas and Georgia Halls of Fame. When *Sports Illustrated* selected its All-Century (collegiate) Team in 1969, Nobis was among those honored. ★

Don Meredith

He came out of the backwoods of East Texas to become a Dallas folk hero, first as a flat-topped All-America quarterback at Southern Methodist and then for nine years as the finger-snapping, good-timing field general of the Dallas Cowboys. They called him Dandy Don, the first bona fide professional sports star the city ever had.

And even if they did see fit to boo him on occasional Sundays w h e n his passes wobbled incomplete and his play selection was singled out as the primary reason certain defeats were snatched from the jaws of victory, all would be forgiven on Monday and he would find himself invited to another round of Big D social events. Don Meredith, with his folksy talk, his Sunday School manners and the kind of good looks that caused normally poised debutantes to have sweaty palms, reigned as Dallas' man about town during his residence.

And despite the fact he never guided the Cowboys into a Super Bowl or claimed the NFL passing title, Meredith is still looked upon today as one of the primary factors in Dallas' emergence from expansion team also-ran to pro football's big time.

Even when his football playing days were past, his accomplishments as an all-around athlete and All-State shrub judger in hometown Mount Vernon, as a two-time All-American at SMU and his career with the Cowboys scrapbook material, Meredith's impact on Texas sports would still be felt. As a broadcaster for ABC's successful Monday Night Football telecasts, he received an Emmy Award.

When, a few years back, he was inducted into the Texas Sports Hall of Fame, the usually flip Dandy Don admitted it was an honor not taken lightly. "It's human nature to want to be highly regarded, to be loved, to be well thought of," he said, "and being picked for such an honor is a tangible thing that says to you that you are well regarded. My days as an athlete are long behind me, but, yes, I would like to think that a few of the things I managed to accomplish won't be forgotten."

Reared in Mount Vernon, Meredith has, in many ways, not strayed all that far from his native land. For all the celebrity he earned as a broadcaster and actor following his playing days, he still holds a strong appreciation for many of life's more uncomplicated things.

In many ways he's still very much the carefree youngster reared by Jeff and Hazel Meredith, hanging around his dad's dry goods store, quarterbacking the Mount Vernon High Tigers, or setting a scoring record of 52 points in a single game in Dallas' Dr Pepper basketball tournament, or performing in one-act plays or being a member of the Future Farmers of America.

Those days also provide positive memories of his athletic past. "In many ways," he said, "the high school days were the most fun. Then, you were just a step above sandlot play and winning and losing wasn't the beginning and end of the world. Maybe we would get our tails whipped by the Bowie Pirates but the next Friday night we'd come back and beat the Atlanta Rabbits and everything would be fine. Those were fun days."

So, too, were his collegiate and pro days—for the most part. He was named to All-America teams in 1958 and '59 while rewriting the Mustangs passing record books.

Then came the birth of the Cowboys, and Meredith was quickly signed to a personal services contract by owner Clint Murchison even before the new NFL franchise was up and running.

"There were," Meredith said, "a lot of fun times, a lot of good times."

There is, of course, a regret or two. "If I had it all to do over again, I'd really like to have won the NFL passing title. I had a chance to do it one year and went out in the last game of the season and completed one of nine—and the only reason that one was complete was because the wind blew it back into the field of play and (Bob) Hayes caught it.

"I could have wrapped up the title with just a mediocre day, but I blew it. Looking back, I have to think maybe I was a little afraid of winning it, afraid of some of the responsibilities and expectations that might have gone with winning the title."

Today, in retrospect, that shortcoming is far over-shadowed by the positives of his career. ★

Jerry LeVias

It is difficult to believe in today's social climate, but when the landmark event occurred four decades ago it took an unrivaled measure of bold courage and willingness to challenge a too-longstanding Southwest Conference tradition. For all of its treasured football history of national championships, Heisman Trophy winners, and endless lists of All-American performers, the league had held stubbornly to a "No Blacks Allowed" stance. Until innovative Southern Methodist coach Hayden Fry and a dynamic and diminutive Beaumont high school standout named Jerry LeVias joined forces to bring about change.

In the summer of 1965, LeVias, a highly regarded quarterback for Beaumont's Hebert High School, accepted an invitation from Fry and SMU, thus becoming the league's first African American player to receive an athletic scholarship. And, while the coach and player would initially face a barrage of cruel taunts, angry criticism and even death threats for their respective decisions, the pioneering effort ultimately paid dividends that reached far beyond the Saturday heroics of LeVias and the sudden success of the team he played for.

Jerry LeVias would not only earn All-America honors and help bring the Mustangs their first conference title in 18 years; he paved the way for others, leading what would become a long parade of once-ignored athletes into an arena previously denied them.

Certainly he came to the task with an impressive résumé. At Hebert he had excelled in the classroom as well as on the athletic field. No doubt about his genes: cousins Mel and Miller Farr went on to standout college and professional careers. Speed? He was a part of the school's state championship 440-yard relay. It was, however, on the football field that young LeVias really raised eyebrows. Like during a 21-8 victory over arch rival Booker T. Washington, when he scored all three of his team's touchdowns on runs of over 70 yards.

Impressive indeed for a young man who, at age 12, had suffered a stroke that had briefly left him unable to walk. It took five years for him to completely recover, causing his mother to forbid him to play high school football. LeVias assured her he would act only as the team's manager. In reality he was scoring 26 touchdowns for Hebert as a junior, then 17 as a senior.

If there was concern

that he might not succeed at the collegiate level it was only because of his size. When LeVias enrolled at SMU, he stood 5'9" and weighed 177 pounds. It would be an issue rarely mentioned during a career in which, playing wide receiver and returning kicks for the Mustangs, he was named All-Southwest Conference three times and in his senior season was a unanimous choice to All-American teams picked for both athletic achievement as well as academics. By the time he completed his eligibility, he had rewritten the school's record books: career receiving yardage (2,275), catches (155) and touchdowns (22). In a 1968 game against powerhouse Ohio State, LeVias caught 15 passes.

Invited to post-season all-star games, he was selected the Most Valuable Player in the Senior Bowl and American Bowl.

The impact LeVias could have on a game is mirrored in a report filed by longtime Associated Press writer Harold Ratliff: "Jerry LeVias was in on only 66 plays in 1966 (his sophomore season) but accomplished more than any other player in the Southwest Conference. He was credited with winning six of SMU's eight victories. He did it all while playing end, making runs on end-around plays, throwing passes, catching passes, returning punts and kickoffs. . . . "

Texas Tech coach J. T. King called LeVias the greatest big-play man he'd seen since the glory days of SMU's Heisman winner Doak Walker.

Still, for all his accomplishments, there were those who insisted LeVias was too small to advance his career into the professional ranks. At the end of the 1969 NFL season, Houston Oiler wide receiver LeVias, a second-round draft selection, was named Rookie of the Year after leading his team in receptions as well as punt and kickoff return yardage.

LeVias spent two seasons with the Oilers before being traded to the San Diego Chargers where he played another four years.

In 2003, he was inducted into the National College Football Hall of Fame where he told the audience, "I look back on it all," LeVias says, "and a lot of what I went through as a young man now seems funny. But I've drawn strength from everything that happened. It was definitely my faith in God—and in people—that helped me along." ★

Y. A. Tittle

Yelberton Abraham Tittle, Jr.'s name was, to the good fortune of sports pages everywhere, abbreviated simply to Y.A. early in his growing up days in Marshall, Texas, thus saving journalists considerable space as they chronicled his long-running career as one of football's most accomplished quarterbacks. His résumé would grow to mind-blowing proportions, from his days as a stellar schoolboy tailback for the Marshall High Mavericks to all-conference recognition at Louisana State University, then 17 years as a coast-to-coast NFL standout and eventual inductee into the Hall of Fame. His mind-blowing pro ball statistics (28,339 yards passing, 212 touchdowns thrown) alone were enough to assure him a proud place in the game's history.

However, if one goes deep enough into Tittle's athletic achievements, he'll locate yet another grand title: Strike-breaker, savior of the 1947 Cotton Bowl.

It was the year that 9-1 LSU, ranked No. 8 in the nation, was invited to Dallas to play the University of Arkansas in the New Year's Day affair. Following tradition, the Bengals players were told that Cotton Bowl officials would provide each player with $200 expense money for their stay in Dallas. The players felt the stipend should be more. They held a meeting, voted to request no less than $300, and approached LSU officials with their demand. They were turned down flatly and were angered to a point where they began discussing a strike. Stubbornly, they talked of neither continuing to practice nor play the Cotton Bowl game.

Tittle was among a small group of players who had not been in favor of the stance. And finally, with tempers at boiling point, he called a meeting and urged his teammates to play the game. In years to come, he pointed out, the amount of spending money they received would be forgotten; that they had played in a major bowl game would remain with them forever. His speech and leadership saved the day.

And on New Year's Day, LSU and 14-point underdog Arkansas fought to the only 0-0 tie in the game's storied history. Playing in rain, sleet and 20-degree temperatures, Tittle passed for 271 yards, driving the Bengals inside the Arkansas 10-yard line four times. The Razorbacks, however, refused to allow a score. Still, for his efforts, Tittle was named the game's Most Valuable Player.

It would be the first in a long line of such honors.

The athletic journey of Tittle was a coast-to-coast

trip. Heavily recruited during his senior year at Marshall, he signed a letter of agreement to attend LSU but, in the eleventh hour, was persuaded by legendary University of Texas coach Blair Cherry to enroll at the Austin school. Upon his arrival he learned that Texas had already signed a gifted young schoolboy quarterback named Bobby Layne. And while the two became friends and roommates, Tittle neither warmed to the UT atmosphere or the idea that he might spend his collegiate career playing behind Layne. An LSU assistant coach drove to Austin, picked Tittle up, and spirited him away to a brilliant tenure as quarterback of the Bengals.

From the collegiate ranks, Tittle launched his professional career with a two-year stay as quarterback of the Baltimore Colts, members of the old All-America Football Conference. When the league disbanded in 1950, he joined the San Francisco 49ers for whom he played for a decade. Yet despite being selected to the Pro Bowl four times and honored as the NFL's Most Valuable Player in 1957, he was constantly in battle with first Frankie Albert, then John Brodie for the starting position.

In 1960 he was traded to the New York Giants. There, he blossomed, leading the Giants to three straight Eastern Division championships, again earning league MVP honors in 1962 and '63.

By the time he called it a career, Tittle had rewritten the NFL record book with his celestial passing yardage. In a 49-34 win over Washington in 1962, he threw for seven touchdowns. That year, his 36 TD passes established a league record. He was the first NFL quarterback in league history to throw for 30 touchdowns in consecutive seasons.

"Going to the Giants," he wrote in his autobiography, *I Pass,* "was the greatest thing that ever happened to me as an athlete."

Still, he left the game with one goal unfulfilled. During his lengthy and celebrated career, Tittle never led a team to an NFL championship.

That shortcoming, however, was no cause for fret on the part of the voters for NFL Hall of Fame membership. Nor was it a factor when the Giants organization retired his jersey number 14.

And, he and wife Minnette did his sons a favor. Having spent a lifetime explaining why his name was Yelberton Abraham Tittle, Jr., he named them Pat and Mike. ★

Tim Brown

It is one of those marvelous sports trivia questions whose answer dumbfounds most: Name the only public high school in the United States to produce two Heisman Trophy winners. Answer: Dallas' Woodrow Wilson High.

Earlier in this little book you read about the remarkable exploits of TCU quarterback Davey O'Brien, winner of college football's highest honor in 1938. Forty-nine years later, the award was accepted by Notre Dame's Tim Brown, also a Woodrow Wilson graduate. For good measure, Brown also became the first wide receiver ever to win the Heisman. That same year he would, just as O'Brien had a half century earlier, also receive the Walter Camp Award as the country's top collegiate player.

Not bad for someone whose career seemed destined to more defeats than victories. During his three years as a starter for Woodrow Wilson, the ever-struggling Wildcats could do no better than a 4-25-1 record. Still colleges nationwide sought the services of the talented all-purpose player. Next stop, Notre Dame, where, alas, the fortunes were only slightly better. The Fighting Irish, despite weekly heroics that earned Brown the nickname "Touchdown Timmy," posted a 25-21 record during his four-year stay and went 0-2 in bowl game appearances.

That record, however, was hardly a reflection of the efforts of the two-time All-American. As a four-year starter, playing wide receiver and returning kicks, he had 137 receptions, established a school record with 5,024 all-purpose yards, and accounted for 22 touchdowns.

Then, as a rookie with the NFL Oakland Raiders, the 6'0," 195-pound receiver continued his record-setting pace. The sixth pick in the 1988 draft, Brown led the league in kickoff returns, return yardage and yards-per-return. He would also lead the NFL in punt returns in 1994 and in receptions in '97. Selected to the Pro Bowl nine times and named All-Pro on seven occasions,

he ultimately surpassed Raiders legend Gene Upshaw's franchise endurance record by playing in 224 games.

For all his remarkable accomplishments, however, there would be no championship ring. The Raiders, a team that seemed in constant turmoil generated by controversial general manager Al Davis, repeatedly fell short. Even when the team did advance into the playoffs, disappointment awaited. In 1990, they lost to Buffalo in the AFC championship game. The following year they were eliminated in the first round wildcard playoffs. In '93 the Bills again beat them, this time in the division playoffs. In 2000 and 2001 they were eliminated in the conference title game by the Baltimore Ravens, then in the divisional round by the New England Patriots.

Finally, in 2002, Tim Brown and the Raiders made it to Super Bowl XXXVII and were favored to defeat NFC champion Tampa Bay. As usual, controversy was the order of the day. A year earlier, the unpredictable Davis had offered the rights to his coach, Jon Gruden, to the Bucs in exchange for four high draft choices and $8 million. Tampa Bay jumped at the opportunity. Thus the championship game would be labeled the "Gruden Bowl," matching the young coach's "new team" against his "old team." Clearly, he harbored no sentimental feelings for his former employer Davis.

The game's outcome was never in doubt as Tampa Bay dominated, intercepting Raiders quarterback Rich Gannon five times enroute to a surprisingly easy 48-21 victory. Once again, Brown's chance at being a member of a championship team had slipped away.

51

Following the 2003 season, his sixteenth with the Raiders, he was released and quickly signed by Gruden and Tampa Bay. And in a touch of sweet irony, it was against his old Raiders team that Brown made his landmark 100th career touchdown catch early in the 2004 season.

Named to the NFL's All-Decade Team, Brown retired after one season with the Buccaneers, leaving behind a remarkable record: During his lengthy career he caught 1,094 passes for 14,934 yards and 100 touchdowns. Additionally, he'd returned punts for 3,320 yards and kickoffs for 1,235, giving him a total of 19,682 all-purpose yards.

Some of which, no doubt, he would have happily exchanged for just one championship season. ★

Ed Sprinkle

He arrived on the Abilene campus of little Hardin-Simmons in the fall of 1940, woefully uneducated in the finer points of football. Before attempting to play the game at the collegiate level, Ed Sprinkle's entire athletic résumé included a single season of six-man football in the West Texas hamlet of Tuscola. He'd never even seen a college game.

When, in fact, his coach instructed him to work at the tackle position in his first collegiate practice, Sprinkle had to ask where he was to line up. Hardly a predictor of future greatness.

Still, he played at a small school All-American level for the Texas school until World War II forced Hardin-Simmons to discontinue its football program since so many of its players, Sprinkle included, were marching off to war. Enlisting in the navy, he received an appointment to the Naval Academy where he played for the Midshipmen in the 1943 season.

Jump ahead now to the late '40s and early '50s and check the Sprinkle highlights: four invitations to the Pro Bowl as a member of the Chicago Bears and selection to the NFL's All-Decade team. For good measure, the title of the "meanest man in football" was bestowed on him in a 1950 *Collier's* magazine profile.

Legendary Bears coach George Halas, who had signed Sprinkle to a $7,200-per-season contract after the war, would later second *Collier's* motion, remembering Sprinkle as the toughest player he ever coached.

"I was really surprised to hear that Halas had said that," Sprinkle admits. "I think everyone was expecting him to say (NFL Hall of Fame linebacker) Dick Butkus.

"You know, there was a time when in the minds of a lot of people that 'toughest player' and 'meanest player' business translated to 'dirty player.' I was never a dirty player. I played rough and hard–but not dirty. My job was to get past offensive linemen who were usually a lot bigger than I was and create havoc in the backfield."

He did so with a vengeance.

Playing for the Bears from 1944 through 1955, he began his pro career as an offensive guard but later spent a decade as a two-way performer at offensive and defensive end. And, while he did catch 10 passes in his career, it was on defense that he excelled, earning four invitations to the Pro Bowl and playing a key role in Chicago's 1946 NFL championship season.

The 24-14 victory over the New York Giants in the championship game, he says, provided his greatest moment as an athlete.

Today a member of the Helms Foundation Hall of Fame, the Chicago Bears Hall of Fame and the Hardin-Simmons Hall of Fame, Sprinkle laughs off the stories that accompanied his legendary reputation.

The cross-town rival Chicago Cardinals, he suggests, were responsible for much of the folklore. "They once said I intentionally stepped on the chest of one of their offensive lineman," Sprinkle remembers. "Never happened. Sure, I went over him to get to the quarterback, but I never stepped on him. Then there was the story that they (the Cardinals) decided not to block me and just let me through the line so the quarterback Paul Christman could hit me in the face with a pass. That never happened, either—unless Christman's pass missed me.

"I do, however, remember being in a big pile at the end of a play and their running back Charlie Trippi hitting me in the face, then taking off toward the sideline," he told the *Chicago Sun-Times.*

All that aside, Sprinkle says, he, Trippi and Christman became close friends once their playing careers were over. "That's just the way we played the game back then. We played hard and respected each other."

Controversy, however, seemed always to be Sprinkle's companion. At the beginning of one season, Wilson Sporting Goods had developed a new style helmet which Sprinkle liked far better than the one he'd worn in years past. In the first game he wore it, several players he rushed past to make tackles were forced to leave the game with injuries of varying degrees. Finally, a referee stopped the game and asked to examine Sprinkle's helmet. He ruled it illegal and rolled it toward Coach Halas on the sidelines.

Halas, rolled the helmet back. This exchange went on several times until the official informed the Bears coach that Sprinkle would not be allowed to continue the game if he insisted on wearing the new helmet.

"I got my old one and the game went on," Sprinkle remembers. The following week, after a league meeting on the matter, the new helmet the Bears defender had debuted was ruled legal and players throughout the NFL immediately switched to it.

"As far as I know," Sprinkle says, "that was the one and only time that a helmet was thrown out of a game."

Raymond Berry

There are athletes born to greatness, others who are self-made. Had one bet on Raymond Berry becoming one of football's legendary receivers it would have been judged a fool's wager. This was, remember, a young man who didn't even earn a starting position on Paris High School's varsity, a team his father coached, until his senior year. One leg was shorter than the other, forcing him to wear special shoes. His eyesight was poor and the word "speed" was never mentioned when his short list of abilities was tallied.

At Southern Methodist, he caught only 33 passes in his three seasons as a Mustang. When time came for the 1954 NFL draft, many were surprised that he was a twentieth-round pick of the Baltimore Colts—selected only after the names of 231 other collegiate players had been called. Surely if life intended the Corpus Christi-born Berry stardom, it was in some other line of pursuit.

Yet through sheer determination and an obsessive attention to the minute details of his craft, Berry forged a record-breaking professional career that ultimately led to his induction into the Pro Football Hall of Fame. During his 13 years with the Colts, he led the league in receptions three times (1958-59-60), earning All-Pro recognition in each of those years, was invited to participate in six Pro Bowls, and played a major role in his team's winning two league titles.

In the famed 1958 NFL Championship game against the New York Giants—still considered by many pro football historians as the greatest game ever played—he made a playoff record 12 catches for 178 yards. And during the Colts' game-winning drive in overtime, Berry made two key receptions that set the stage for fullback Alan Ameche's victorious plunge into the end zone.

Before nor since has there been a receiver who ran such precise routes. In preparation for each game, he urged famed Colts quarterback Johnny Unitas to remain on the practice field long after others had headed for the locker room. Repeatedly, Berry ran perfect routes, making catches with boring regularity. While other receivers often reported for early pre-game warm-ups dressed in shorts and t-shirt, Berry, keenly concerned with timing, always ran his routes in full uniform.

During one training camp practice, the story goes, he ran a sideline pattern and made the catch only after stepping out of bounds. Briefly halting practice, he insisted to the Colts coaching staff that the width of the practice field was a foot or so short of regulation. Coaches scoffed but Berry held his ground until, finally, a tape was hauled out and the width of the field was measured. Berry, the perfectionist, was right.

Berry insisted that he had, over the course of his playing days, developed no fewer that 88 different moves to break away from defenders and get open.

During Berry's NFL career, he caught a then-record 631 passes for 9,275 yards and scored 68 touchdowns. Impressive statistics all. But they pale when compared to one he prides most: Only one time in 13 professional seasons, did he fumble.

And the legend of Raymond Berry would not end following his retirement at the end of the 1967 season. In 1973 he entered the Hall of Fame and his jersey number 82 was retired by the Colts. When the 1950s NFL Team of the Decade was selected, Berry was among its members.

Then, in 1984, he became head coach of the New England Patriots and guided his team into Super Bowl XX against the Chicago Bears. The Bears, considered one of the greatest teams in modern NFL history, defeated Berry's Patriots, 46-10. Before ending his coaching career, Berry fashioned a 48-39 won-lost record. ★

Harley Sewell

The nostalgia merchants would have loved St. Jo, Texas, in the late '40s. It was a 900 population farming hamlet where high school football was the primary source of entertainment and two dozen members in good standing of the Fighting Panthers were teenaged pillars of the community.

Primary among those legendary figures who carried the St. Jo High banner was Harley Sewell, a big, blond farmer's son who daily walked or hitchhiked the eight miles from Tyler's Bluff to play fullback and serve as captain of the '48 Panthers team. And while his high school heroics hardly caused college recruiters to scurry for the nearest road map, they did account for a number of Friday night celebrations.

Truth is, no college was aware of his rare and raw talent until a local gentleman farmer, who had earned his degree at the University of Texas, made a phone call. In nearby Wichita Falls, the annual summer Oil Bowl, matching the premier graduating seniors from Texas and Oklahoma high schools, was to be played. Coaching the Texas squad was the staff of the University of Texas. When the caller suggested there was a "big ol' rawboned kid over in St. Jo they should take a look at," one of the UT coaches suggested that Sewell come over to Wichita Falls for a visit.

The following day, dressed in T-shirt and overalls, the 17-year-old Sewell knocked on a hotel room door and was greeted by then assistant coach J. T. King.

"I'm looking for the Texas football coach," the shy Sewell announced.

"I'm one of them," King replied.

There were a few seconds of stunned silence as Sewell shook his head before responding. "My gawd," he said, "how many ya'll got?"

There are countless such stories still told about Harley Sewell, who grew into an All-American lineman for the University of Texas in the early '50s, then enjoyed a 10-year professional career with the Detroit Lions.

"You know," he said, "I seem to get a little better every year. Or at least the stories I hear making the rounds make it seem that way. The truth is, college football players of my day weren't even close to being as good as today's players. Those who insist on making comparisons between today's players and those of my generation must have awful short memories."

61

Modesty, then, is also part of the Sewell legacy.

The adjustment from North Texas farmhouse to the athletic dorm at Texas was no small task for Sewell. Assistant coach King recalls getting a call from Harley's roommate one morning, telling him that a distraught Sewell was packing to return to St. Jo.

"I hurried over to the dorm and, sure enough, he had this beat-up old cardboard suitcase on his bed. I asked what the problem was and he said he was homesick. He'd throw a pair of socks into the suitcase and I'd pitch them back into the drawer. I kept talking to him, pitching his clothes out of the suitcase as fast as he put them in it and finally managed to convince him to stick around."

It was an act of gentle persuasion that was to pay great dividends for the Longhorns' program.

Bully Gilstrap, another Texas assistant at the time, delighted in recalling Sewell as "the best snuff-dipping guard we ever had."

"We were getting ready for the Cotton Bowl one year," King recalls, "and I was sitting at home one evening when this alumnus called to say he'd just found out that Harley dipped snuff and wanted to know what kind of disciplinary measures we were planning.

"I tried to convince the guy that Harley had probably just tried it as a lark but he was having none of it, saying he'd been told Harley had dipped snuff since his high school days, and again asked what action we were going to take for so drastic a violation of training rules.

"Finally, I'd had all of the guy I wanted so I suggested he do some investigating for me. That really excited him and he asked what I wanted him to do. I told him to see if he could find out what brand Harley was using—then I'd recommend it to the entire team. Right after that the phone went dead."

Following his All-American senior season, Sewell was the Detroit Lions' No. 1 selection in the NFL draft, signing a contract that would earn him $6,500 per year. As a bonus, he got to room with another former Longhorn, quarterback Bobby Layne.

By mid-season Sewell was a starter for the Lions team that would win the NFL championship. So impressed with his rookie showing were Detroit officials that he was awarded a $250 raise. After 10 years, four Pro Bowl appearances and two league championships, Sewell was traded to the Los Angeles Rams in 1963. In his fourth game with his new team he was carried off the field with a vertebra pressing against a nerve in his spine. Doctors told him his playing days were over.

Despite the fact the Rams were obligated to pay him for the entire season even if his career was over, Sewell approached team owner Dan Reeves, asking if there was something he could do to earn his keep. He suggested that he might be able to lend a hand to the Rams scouting department.

"In all my years in the game," Reeves said, "Harley Sewell was the only player ever to approach me with such a proposition. He's a rare kind of person."

For the next two decades, Sewell served as a player scout for the Rams. ★

Eric Dickerson

Even as a celebrated schoolboy athlete in little Sealy, Texas, he had a smooth, gliding running style that looked almost effortless. College recruiters nationwide coveted the services of the 6'3," 230-pound All-State youngster who could run the 100-yard dash in 9.4. And, as coaches from all of the big name university programs came to call, Eric Dickerson's mother carefully listened to their pitches and promises, then made her son's decision for him.

While Eric was enamored of the high profile schools like the University of Oklahoma and Texas A&M, his mother judged Southern Methodist University and its coach Ron Meyer the best fit for her talented offspring. It was a judgment that paid great dividends for the Mustangs.

Teaming with fellow blue chip recruit Craig James to form a running duo the media nicknamed the Pony Express, Dickerson helped lift SMU football into national prominence. Before his collegiate career ended he had gained 4,450 yards on 790 carries, erasing the Southwest Conference records of Texas' Heisman Trophy winner Earl Campbell. His 48 touchdowns tied the long-standing SMU record set by the immortal Doak Walker. Twice he was named to All-America teams, finished third in the Heisman balloting following his senior year, and was the first round NFL draft pick of the Los Angeles Rams.

And again it was his mom who pointed the way. The Los Angeles Express of the newly-formed United States Football League had lobbied hard for his services, keenly aware that a player of his stature could provide the league instant star power. In the end, however, it would be Mrs. Dickerson's firm urging that he play in the established NFL.

It was in the professional ranks that the long-striding Dickerson took center stage. No longer sharing the role with alternate James (who went off to stardom with the Washington Federals of the USFL, then the NFL New England Patriots), he took dead aim on the NFL record books. In his first year as a pro he was named Rookie of the Year, All-Pro and was invited to the Pro Bowl after rushing for 1,808 yards and scoring 18 touchdowns. It was but a preview of what was to come.

In his second season with the Rams he rushed for 100 yards or more in 11 games, breaking the record formerly held by Hall of Famer O. J. Simpson. Dickerson's 2,105 yards rushing in 1984 vaulted him past yet another Simpson mark. Big games became commonplace. In a playoff game against the Dallas Cowboys, he rushed for a record 248 yards. In his five years with the Rams, the gifted young Texan collected every plaudit available, including NFL Player of the Year.

Following a lengthy contract dispute, Dickerson was traded to the Indianapolis Colts during the strike-shortened 1987 season. And didn't slow a step. Though appearing in but nine games for the Colts, he still managed to gain 1,011 yards and help his new team into the playoffs for the first time in a decade.

Then, in 1988 he became the first Colts player to lead the league in rushing since the legendary Alan Ameche had accomplished the feat in 1955. By the end of the '89 season he had rushed for 1,000 yards or more in seven straight seasons and reached the 10,000-yard mark after playing in only 91 games.

In time, however, Dickerson was again locked in a contract dispute despite the fact he was the league's highest paid running back. In '92, the Colts traded him to the Los Angeles Raiders. There, his impact was far from what it had been in his glory days. In 16 games, he rushed for only 729 yards and scored but two touchdowns.

He would end his 11-year NFL career in the '93 season as a backup for the Atlanta Falcons, appearing in just four games.

It would, however, be those earlier workhorse days that Pro Football Hall of Fame voters would recall when they chose him for induction with the Class of 1999. ★

Kenneth Hall

The old stadium sat at the far end of a tree-shaded street, drenched in the sweet nostalgic scent of lantana

and honeysuckle, and was once the focal point of the community's social activity. In the early '50s, the 2,000 residents of the community owned two loyalties: to the Imperial Sugar Company, which paid most people's salaries, and the green-and-white-clad Sugar Land High School Gators, a Class B schoolboy dynasty of the time.

During a three-year stretch it won 34 of 36 games and, said retired coach L.V. Hightower, "People from all over came to watch our games." And they entered the stadium with the same question: "What's *his* number?"

Their question referred to No. 31, a 6'1," 205-pound tailback named Kenneth Hall; a gifted, multi-talented athlete many still call the greatest schoolboy football player in Texas history. The proof to the argument can be found in the national high school record books where from 1950 to '53, he climbed to the top in a dozen categories.

The numbers seem more fantasy than fact:

Most points scored in a career—899; most points in a season—395; most career touchdowns—127; most yards rushing in a career—11,232; most yards rushing in a season—4,045; rushing average per game—337.1; most 100-yard games in a career—38; and most consecutive 100-yard games—21.

He also kicked 137 extra points and passed for 3,326 yards during his freshman-to-senior statistical binge. His 520 yards rushing in a single game stood as a record until 1974 when John Bunch of Elkins, Arizona, rushed for 608. Bunch's performance, it should be noted, came after 38 carries in a game which saw him on the field until the final gun. Hall, on the other hand, accomplished his 520 yards (and seven touchdowns) on just 11 carries—that's 47.3 yards per carry—and retired to the bench after just two quarters.

When he wasn't breaking for long distance runs from scrimmage, he was adding to his total yardage with a 64-yard kickoff return, an 82-yard punt return, and a 21-yard return with an interception. By the time the Gators had claimed their 73-14 victory over an outclassed Houston Lutheran High, Hall had amassed 687 total yards in just 30 minutes of play.

"There's no telling how many points he would have scored or yards he might have gained had we let him play the whole game against some of the weaker opponents we faced," said Hightower. "We had to take him out to keep from embarrassing some of the schools we played.

"There are people quick to assume that Kenneth's records were made against a lot of inferior teams, but that was hardly the case. Hall could make a very good team look bad."

The coach told of a game against Orchard High, a better-than-average team that had taken the opening kickoff and marched downfield for a score. Moments later Sugar Land had the ball on its own 20-yard line.

Hall swept to his left and went 80 yards for an apparent touchdown. Except for the fact officials ruled that a Gators lineman had been offside. After a five-yard penalty Hall ran the same play for an apparent touchdown. But there had been another penalty flag.

Hightower recalls that one of the referees called for a

time out after Hall's second run. "I need a break," the official explained. "That Number 31 is running me to death."

In addition to his football heroics, Hall was also a starter for the Gators basketball team and twice led Sugar Land to the state track and field championship, scoring 38 points at the meet his sophomore year and 36 in his junior season. He ran the 100-yard dash in 9.7, the 220 in 21.4 and the 440 in 49 flat. He long jumped 23 feet and put the shot 53 feet, handled the anchor leg on the Gators 440-yard relay and occasionally threw the discus and high jumped. Though injured in his senior year, he still managed to win a silver medal in the shot put.

When Hall's school day records are recited, Hightower pointed out, one of the most impressive is often overlooked. In four years he scored 83 points at the state track and field meet.

And, so, whatever happened to the boy known as the Sugar Land Express? Why no collegiate records after receiving a scholarship from the legendary Paul (Bear) Bryant at Texas A&M?

If the judgment of Bryant is to be believed, Ken Hall couldn't—or wouldn't—play defense at a time when all Aggie starters were expected to be two-way performers. In Bryant's scheme, his fullback was also his middle linebacker. When he and the Sugar Land youngster couldn't agree on the matter, Hall left college.

For a time he played professionally for the Edmonton Eskimos of the Canadian League, then later played briefly with the St. Louis Cardinals of the NFL and returned kicks for the Houston Oilers for a season.

Today, Hall rarely speaks of those days when he was deemed the greatest high school running back in the country.

"Really, it's just a blur to me now," he says. "There comes a time when you put all those things behind you." ★

Afterword

And so, as we come to the end of this little nostalgic journey, I can already hear the rumble. Texas A&M faithfuls are wondering why there are so dang many University of Texas players included and an arm-long list of Aggie legends were overlooked.

And, no doubt, they're not the only ones complaining.

How, for the love of Pete, could you leave out TCU and San Diego Chargers running back LaDainian Tomlinson? What kind of blithering idiot knuckleheaded jerk would compile a list that leaves off not one but *two* Texas-born and raised Heisman Trophy winners—Hooks and the University Oklahoma star Billy Sims and Midland and UT ex Ricky Williams?

Ever heard of Kyle Rote (SMU) or Scott Appleton (Texas), Dickie Moegle (Rice) or Mike Singletary (Baylor)? Forget about Mean Joe Greene who went from Temple to North Texas to the Super Bowl champion Pittsburgh Steelers? How about Clyde (Bulldog) Turner who came out of West Texas to become one of the greatest Chicago Bears players in history?

And, Mr. Hot-Shot Sportswriter, that's just the beginning of the most glaring omissions. Don't get me started.

If you weren't so all-fired hung up on places of birth, you could have written the whole book about great Cowboys players; the Staubachs, Aikmans, Smiths and Dorsetts, just to mention a few who certainly spent enough blood and sweat on Texas soil to earn their citizenships.

But, what the hey, you did make *some* good picks.

And, if you read carefully, it has provided a few dandy trivia questions. Like, for instance: Name two NFL Hall of Fame quarterbacks who began their college careers at the University of Texas but never played a down. Answer: Sammy Baugh and Y. A. Tittle.

Seems to me that little-known fact alone should be worth the cover price. ★

Photo credits

Sammy Baugh. *Courtesy TCU.*

Raymond Berry. *Courtesy SMU Athletic Public Relations.*

Tim Brown. *Courtesy University of Notre Dame.*

Earl Campbell. *Courtesy University of Texas.*

Eric Dickerson. *Courtesy SMU Athletic Public Relations.*

Kenneth Hall. *Courtesy the Texas Sports Hall of Fame in Waco, Texas.*

John Kimbrough. *Courtesy Texas A&M University.*

Bobby Layne. *Courtesy University of Texas.*

Jerry LeVias. *Courtesy SMU Athletic Public Relations.*

Bob Lilly. *Courtesy TCU.*

Don Meredith. *Courtesy Dallas Cowboys.*

Tommy Nobis. *Courtesy University of Texas.*

Davey O'Brien. *Courtesy TCU.*

Harley Sewell. *Courtesy University of Texas.*

Ed Sprinkle. *Courtesy Hardin-Simmons University.*

Y. A. Tittle. *Courtesy Louisiana State University.*

Doak Walker. *Courtesy SMU Athletic Public Relations.*

Vince Young. *Courtesy University of Texas.*

Sources

A number of the profiles in this book originally appeared in other publications under the author's byline, though in different forms. Stowers wrote about Sammy Baugh for the *Abilene Reporter News,* Earl Campbell for the Sunday magazine of the *Dallas Morning News,* John Kimbrough for the *Houston Chronicle,* Don Meredith for *Country Rambler,* Bobby Layne and Harley Sewell for the UT alumni magazine *Alcalde,* Bob Lilly for *Dallas Cowboys* magazine, Davey O'Brien for the *Dallas Morning News,* and Ken Hall for *Sports Illustrated.* For material used in other chapters, the author nods sincere thanks to the archives of the Pro Football Hall of Fame, College Football Hall of Fame, Wikipedia, and SI.com. Also of great help were *What It Means to be a Longhorn* by Bill Little and Jenna McEachern, Dan Jenkins' *I'll Tell You One Thing,* Y.A. Tittle's *I Pass,* and Witt Channing's *Doak Walker: More Than a Hero.* ★

About the Author

Carlton Stowers is the author of over two dozen non-fiction books, including *To The Last Breath* and *Careless Whispers,* both winners of the Mystery Writers of America's Edgar Award, and *Within These Walls* (with the Reverend Carroll Pickett), which received the Writers League of Texas' Violet Crown Award. His sports writing was included in the *Best American Sports Writing of 2004.* Stowers is a member of the Texas Institute of Letters and in 2007 was the recipient of the A.C. Greene Literary Award. He resides in Cedar Hill, Texas. ★

Texas Football Legends
Greats of the Game

ISBN 978-0-87565-376-1
Case. $8.95

A TEXAS SMALL BOOK
★

ISBN 978-0-87565-376-1

5 0 8 9 5

9 780875 653761